DEBORAH AMSBERRY

Jerome, Arizona: The Wickedest Town in the Wild West

This book was professionally typeset on Reedsy.
Find out more at reedsy.com

I dedicate this little book to my amazing husband Lanny.
Without his love, encouragement, and support, I would never have realized
my dreams of becoming a writer. He has been with me every step of my
journey with a smile, positive comments, and most of all his love.
I love you.
Deb

Contents

1

Introduction

When the American West was still wild, no town was more wild and wicked than Jerome, Arizona. This mining town was full of rowdy outlaws, brothels, and gambling halls. The heavy drinking, gambling, brawling, and frolicking with the soiled doves went on around the clock.

The town's riches attracted many fortune seekers; miners came from around the world to seek their fortune. But life in Jerome was difficult, and most prospectors journeyed into these remote regions with nothing more than a mule, a pick, and a shovel. Their disappointments and hardships often led to violence and failure.

In its heyday, Jerome was a bustling mining town. It was home to saloons, gambling halls, brothels, and famous madams. Its streets were often the scene of drunken brawls and gunfights. The town had a reputation for being rowdy and dangerous; it was nicknamed the "The Wickedest Town in the Wild West."

The Jerome mines were the site of the district's smelting operations from

1915 to 1950 and are now a National Historic Landmark. Precariously perched on the slopes of Cleopatra Hill at 5,200 ft, these old gold mining sites provide an expansive view over one helluva valley. Buildings are perched on a 30-degree incline hanging on for dear life and many are still there today.

Jerome was incorporated in 1899, making it the fourth-largest town in Arizona. It is located about 100 miles north of Phoenix along the winding State Route 89A between Sedona and Prescott. It is known as "America's Most Vertical City" with good reason since it is perched on the Cleopatra Hills at an elevation of 5,000 feet.

Despite its checkered past, Jerome is now a fascinating ghost town with many haunted establishments. Its rich history is a story of the American West at its best and worst. This is the perfect destination if you're looking for a place full of mystery and intrigue.

From the mining town days to the current tourist destination, Jerome has always been a place with a bit of an edge. And, if the rumors are true, it's also one of the most haunted towns in America.

2

Jerome the Early Days

Native Americans of Jerome, Arizona

The Verde River Valley was home to many battles between Native Americans and white settlers.

The first people to settle in and around Jerome were the Hohokam tribe; other Native American tribes soon joined them. These tribes did not mine for copper, but they were aware of it; instead, they used the reddish ores to apply color to themselves, their clothes, and blankets.

After the establishment of the Territorial Government in 1863, and the founding of Prescott, settlers began moving and settling into the territories. Some settled in the area of the Verde River and Clear Creek. It was the ideal spot, rich with fertile bottom land and an abundance of game and fish. It wasn't long before it attracted many more white settlers.

Originally the Indians didn't bother the settlers, but as time went on more and more white settlers intruded on their land they became concerned; concerned that the influx of settlers would deprive them of their land. The Indians began attacking and wreaking havoc on the settlers.

The Indian Removal Act was signed into law by President Andrew Jackson in 1830, granting Jackson funds and authority to remove the Indians by force if necessary. Reservations were created for the Native Americans to live. This law was intended to reduce conflict and allow white settlers moving in by the masses to occupy more of the South and West territories.

In 1875 the first mining claims were staked, along with the site for the mill around Jerome. Cleopatra Hill would become Jerome. At the time, that area was part of an Indian reservation.

Located about 20 miles northeast of Prescott and 15 miles southeast of Camp Verde is Cleopatra Hill. Camp Verde was a U.S. Army post and part of the Camp Verde Indian Reservation. The U.S. government had relocated the local Native American tribes to this reservation to accommodate the white settlers coming into the territory. The Camp

Verde Reservation opened to mining and settlement in 1877 when the federal government forced Native Americans (the Hohokam, Yavapai, and Apache tribes) to relocate to the San Carlos Reservation 180 miles away near Globe, Arizona, making room for the mining community of Jerome to develop.

Jerome was once one of the world's wealthiest high-grade copper ore mining towns. It produced more than a billion dollars in copper, silver, and gold over 70 years. In 1885 they established the first copper mining site, and the bad-boy crowd followed the discovery of gold. The town quickly became a wickedly wild and rowdy tent city boomtown, with over 15,000 people living there at its peak. By the 1920s, Jerome was the fourth-largest city in Arizona.

The wagon road built between Flagstaff and Jerome helped turn the tent city mining town into a mining town with wooden buildings, a post office, four saloons, and electric lighting by 1890.

The mining craze started in the late 1800s when miners discovered rich copper ore deposits in Cleopatra Hill, located in the Black Hills of Yavapai County. The first claims were filed in 1876 by Albert Sieber. Albert was an Indian Scout and if the story is correct, he noticed the paint used by the Indians and suspected that it came from a mineral source. Albert followed them up the Verde River where he found red oxide of copper and staked his claim.

Others, such as John Dougherty, John Boyd, Morris Ruffner, and Josiah Riley, also staked claims. Credit for discovering the original United Verde Claims goes to these earliest miners. For the most part, these miners did not have the financial means to develop their holdings for profit, so wealthy investors began buying out these individuals and forming companies with the financial resources to build them.

Morris A. Ruffner was confident in the value of his mine, expecting its worth to be at least a million dollars someday. Keeping his faith in the deal, he partnered with George and Alex McKinnon to develop his mine. But it wasn't enough and soon after the three sold their interests to the then territorial Governor of Arizona, Fredrick A Tritle.

The Territorial Governor, Frederick Tritle, knew he needed financing to pull the copper from the abundant amounts of ore discovered in the mines. That financial support came from two wealthy financiers, James McDonald and Eugene Jerome.

Eugene Murray Jerome

Eugene Jerome was hesitant to get involved but after some coercion from his wife he invested. He asked that the town be named Jerome after him, the wealthy banker who had invested $200,000, but he never saw his name's sake; he never visited once. It is also possible that the $200,000 investment came not from Eugene, but from his wife and sister-in-law as they both had considerable money of their own. There is no straight answer to this.

And yes, the rumors are true Eugene was a cousin of Jeannie Jerome, better known as Lady Randolph Churchill. She was the mother of British prime minister Winston Churchill.

They immediately erected two blast furnaces and worked the mine to a depth of 160 feet for two years, producing high-grade, gold-silver-copper matte. The Santa Fe Railroad was built in Arizona by this time, but the nearest station was still 50 miles away and transportation remained expensive. They had minor successes that didn't last and finances dwindled.

In 1882, Fred Thomas and George Threadwell organized the United Verde Copper Mining Company. They bought the mining claims for $45,000 and established the mining camp that became Jerome. Governor Frederick Tritle maintained an active interest in the company; James McDonald held the position of company president, and Eugene Jerome became the secretary for the United Verde Copper Mining Company.

The United Verde Copper Company was incorporated and began operations in 1883. After building a 50-ton furnace fueled by coke at Jerome and being in operation full-time for four months, United Verde Copper Mine Company processed 5,000 tons of ore, yielding 200 tons of copper bullion and lesser amounts of gold and silver. By the end of the first year, they had produced nearly $800,000 worth of copper and paid $62,000 out in dividends. This success was short-lived; the price of copper began to drop, and by 1884 with financing exhausted, the smelter was closed and remained closed until 1888.

Miners Employed by the United Verde Copper Mining Company in the 1900s

Senator William A. Clark snatched up the property under a lease option on the United Verde Copper Mining Company in 1888 and he purchased it the following year for $80,000. James McDonald was vice president and retained that position until he passed. It was under Clark that the mine finally began to prosper.

Clark was experienced in mining having worked the quartz mines of Colorado in 1862, and then the gold mines of Montana in 1863. He resorted to placer mining in Montana with moderate results. Placer mining was widely used because it was affordable and took advantage of gold's high density; the weight of gold would sink to the bottom of the moving water making it easy to retrieve. It was the main technique used during the early gold rush years.

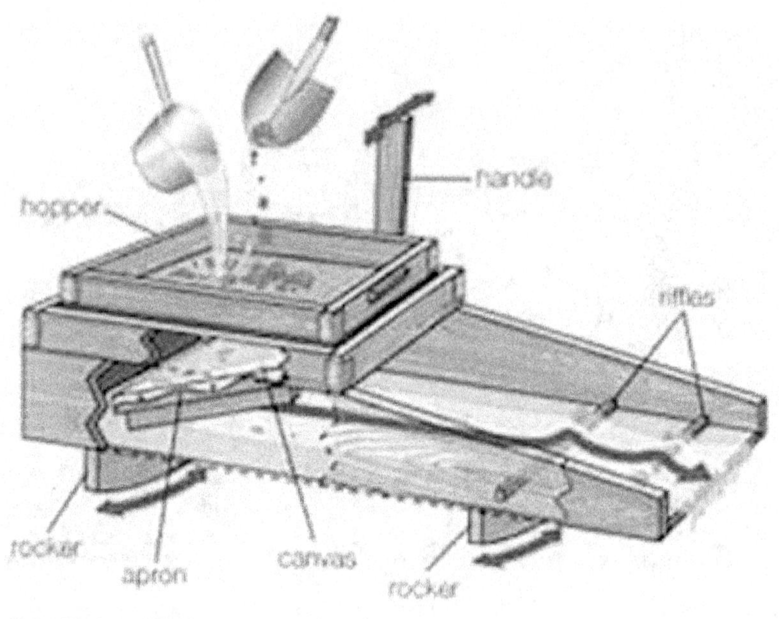

Placer Mining

Clark would change careers several times from miner to banker to politician but always kept a hand in the mining industry.

When he purchased the United Verde Copper Mining Company, Clark began developing the mine to a greater depth and discovered the copper glance ore was 200 ft wide and 600 to 800 feet long. 1894, Clark built a 27-mile narrow-gauge railroad connecting Jerome to the Santa Fe Railroad, making transportation more accessible and less expensive.

The constant shifting and settling of the ground from the mining activity below made it expensive and difficult to maintain the original smelter and mine plant because they were built directly over the mine. In 1912 Clark moved the smelter and mine plant to Clarkdale, about 2,000 feet lower. In Clarkdale larger, more modern 160-ton blast furnaces were constructed. The new Clarkdale plant was completed in May 1915 and drastically reduced expenses. The United Verde Copper Mine Company soon became known as one of the greatest underground mines in the world at a depth of 2500 feet. At its peak, it was producing 15,000,000 pounds of copper per month.

Fires burned for years in the miles of the mine tunnels. Water from recent flooding seeped into the burning tunnels causing an explosion. This happened during a shift change when at least a dozen miners were waiting to be lifted from the mine. They were either killed or seriously injured from the scolding steam and gases. These fires became so widespread and uncontrollable that underground mining was phased out in favor of open-pit mining.

Open-Pit Steam Shovel Mining

Open-pit mining operations started in 1919 and it refers to mining directly from the surface. This method is more practical, cost-effective, and safer than shaft mining.

The "Big Hole" was the name the miners gave to the United Verde Open-Pit Mine.

Under Senator William A Clark, the mine prospered.

Senator William A Clark

Clark held it from 1888-1935, during which time it was probably the wealthiest mine ever worked under individual ownership. Clark owned 95% of the United Verde Copper Company stock, and the remainder was retained by James McDonald, one of the original investors brought in by Governor Fredrick Tritle.

Senator Clark had made approximately $60,000,000 from the mine. His net worth at the time of his death was $150,000,000 which is $2,138,125,867.42 today.

In 1935 the Phelps Dodge Corporation purchased United Verde at the rather steep price of $20.8 million, from Clark's heirs. Phelps Dodge Corporation still owns it today.

Jerome, Arizona, produced wealth from gold, copper, silver, and zinc for over 70 years. The growth and prosperity of these fortunes were dependent on access to eastern markets. The mule-drawn wagons traversing the rough roads to this remote mining camp were replaced by railroads in 1895. The addition of the railroad significantly reduced transportation costs for the mining company.

There were many mines and numerous mining stories, but two primary mines produced more than 99% of the copper production: The United Verde and the United Verde Extension. The United Verde Extension is a story in itself involving The Little Daisy Mine and "Rawhide" Jimmy Douglas.

But the fortune of the town didn't last. By 1930, the mines began to dry up. The Great Depression saw a decline in the price of copper, and Jerome slowly declined into a ghost town. In 1935 the United Verde Copper Mine sold out to Phelps Dodge, who still owns it today. In 1938 the Little Daisy Copper Mine closed.

Phelps Dodge closed the last mine in 1953, ending all primary mining. About $800,000,000 in copper had been removed from the mines by then. The mines closed and Jerome became a veritable ghost town when the population dropped to 50 residents.

T.F. Miller 4-Story Building

Phelps Dodge and the United Verde Companies owned most of the land, and when the mines closed and the population of the town declined, they began bulldozing the buildings. The first to go was the T.F. Miller 4-story building. They paid local kids a penny per brick to remove the mortar from around the brick so it could be reused. In 1956 the demolition was halted by a group of locals who formed the Jerome Historical Society.

3

Jerome's Wicked Wild West Days

Jerome was not all riches and success stories; the town was also full of poverty, crime, violence, and outlaws. Prostitutes walked throughout the city advertising their services. Saloons, gambling halls, brothels, and opium dens were the entertainment along "Prostitute Row."

The town of Jerome, Arizona, is rich with history, some of which are pretty dark and haunted. What made it so famous (or infamous) was its rowdy, wild west past. It was once known as the "Wickedest Town in the Wild West," with danger and adventure lurking around every corner. Jerome has a fascinating history. The town was full of miners looking to strike it rich, and they often spent their hard-earned money on alcohol and women. Prostitute Row was a famous street in Jerome where many of the town's madams plied their trade.

In 1876 copper mining boomed in Jerome. Prostitutes moved in before the miners erected tents. They were labeled "Blanket Whores" because most of their business was conducted outdoors on blankets.

First came the miners to work in the mine, Next came the ladies who lived on the line.

 — Old Western Mining Adage

Prostitute Row and Husband's Alley were notorious for their seedy businesses and crimes. Jerome's red-light district, Prostitute Row was located on the main street and mixed with typical shops like dry goods, mercantile, and jewelry stores. Prostitution, even while illegal, was tolerated in Jerome. Law enforcement would periodically do a sweep to clean up Jerome and force out the prostitutes. Eventually, these businesses were moved off Main Street behind the saloons. Men visiting the bars would enjoy a few drinks, gamble, and then sneak out the back door for more entertainment. Once Prostitute Row was relocated, it was called "Husband's Alley" (where the husband went to cheat on their wives) and the "Old Cribs District."

Men looking primarily for companionship found the classy, expensive ladies in the brothels operated by madams. These ladies were protected and had access to health care, security, and even education. It was not unusual for these ladies to provide nothing more than companionship and conversation for a lonely man. With men outnumbering women 23 to 1, there was no shortage of lonely men starving for female company.

The low-priced ladies lived and worked in the back in the "cribs" of Husband's Alley. Cribs were isolated from the brothels, although some of the madams maintained a string of "cribs" with the girls that were no longer considered desirable for the house. The cribs were identified by red lamps or red curtains hanging in the window. These ladies would service between 30-80 men daily.

Unlike what the stories of the madams of the wild west would have us believe, this was not a glamorous life. These businesswomen were tolerated, not celebrated; they were often scorned, living a life of solitude, loneliness, and danger.

Several madams became rich and famous - this is the story of "Belgian Jennie" Bauters, one of Jerome's more interesting and successful madams who arrived early on the scene when the town was all tents, shacks, and saloons. It has been said that "Belgian Jennie" was the wealthiest madam in Arizona and the first madam of Jerome. She was always charming and generous to her customers.

As the story goes, Jennie was born in 1862 in Belgium and immigrated to America in 1896 as an unmarried woman with a 14-year-old son, Joseph Phillippe. On arrival, Jennie promptly put her son in a Catholic Chicago boarding school where she would visit him from time to time. She then headed to Jerome and the riches that would soon be hers.

Jennie's Place
Belgian Jennie is in the middle wearing black

Jennie's Place, on paper, was a boarding house for women; in reality, it was the grandest brothel in Jerome. Even with the cards stacked against her as an unmarried immigrant, women Jennie managed to acquire a mortgage on three parcels of land. She built a wooden structure and Jennie's Place was born.

Jennie had a knack for this business, and she knew how to engage the men while they waited in the parlor for one of her girls. She knew what to do to make Jennies Place the most desirable to both the clientele and the girls. Unlike the others who made their money renting a room to these girls to perform their services, Jennie provided shelter and protection to her girls as long as they were willing to work.

These soiled doves led dangerous lives, and they had much to fear in their chosen profession. Most would acquire a sexually transmitted disease within a year, not to mention the fear of pregnancy and violence. Jennie offered medical care for her ladies. She offered the miners Black Market Condoms to protect both sides of the transaction. In order to prevent disease and pregnancy. Many miners didn't accept them because they didn't like wearing them. Condoms were made from animal intestines and kept in place with a ribbon tied around the base of their penises. In 1873 the Comstock Law was passed and banned people from sending condoms and other immoral goods through the mail. Condoms went underground to the Black Market.

As the mining population grew, so did Jennie's fortune. Every patron paid the equivalent of one day's mining wages to spend time with her girls. These soiled doves were a fact of life in Jerome. Though they were not technically supposed to be there and were looked down upon by the more proper ladies of the time, they were tolerated as a necessary evil. These ladies tended to dress and behave in ways that were not considered proper. In a town that was short on females, these ladies served an important purpose, providing entertainment and companionship for many lonely men.

Jennie's Place survived three major fires between 1897 and 1900, and each time she rebuilt and continued business as usual. Jennie was a creative thinker and after one of the fires, she offered the men of the town free passes to her girls to rebuild her brothel. The building was up and back in operation in record time.

After the third fire, Jerome incorporated as a city and all buildings had to be fireproof. After the incorporation, Jerome saw women and families moving in, and the brothels were receiving unwanted attention from these so-called respectable citizens.

In 1905, the Jerome Town Council banned women from saloons; after all, this was unheard of in the east, but in 1906 the voters used their power and allowed them back in. In 1913 reformers and these respectable citizens passed an ordinance restricting houses of ill repute from being located downtown on the main street. The bordellos were forced to move off Main Street to Hull Ave, and Husbands Alley was formed; it was the new red-light district. Husbands Alley included the Cribs and the lady's jail. Prostitution was illegal, but that didn't stop the Jerome bordellos; they continued to thrive well into the 1940s.

Jennie saw the writing on the wall and relocated in 1903 to the "The Badlands" of Northern Arizona. With a saloon and two large tents in the back to house her girls and entertain their clients, Jennie started rebuilding her business at the Acme Camp in Goldroad, Arizona, another wild and rowdy mining town

It is here that she met her untimely brutal death at the early age of 44. While still in Jerome, she met a man named Clement C. Leigh. Some say Jennie had taken up with Clement but others say he was harassing and stalking her. Regardless, they both ended up in Northern Arizona. Clement claimed to be her husband, but all records show Jennie as unmarried. It is suspected he was nothing more than a leech looking to part Jennie from her money.

Jennie had voiced many times her fear of Clement, she told anyone who would listen. But it all fell on deaf ears. Clement murdered Jenny in cold blood while several people watched and did nothing. That fateful day Clement was hopped up on alcohol and opium. He wanted Jennie's money to settle a debt, and he was taking that money from her one way or another.

DEATH PENALTY FOR MURDER OF WOMAN

LEIGH FOUND GUILTY OF HOMI-CIDE IN THE FIRST DEGREE.

The man named Leigh, who shot and killed Jennie Bauters at the Gold Roads mining camp in Mohave county on Sunday, September 3, was found guilty of murder in the first degree, and the death penalty affixed by a jury of twelve men in the trial of the case before the district court in Kingman, after ten minutes' deliberation, says the Prescott Journal-Miner.

Leigh, who formerly lived in Jerome, was a very quarrelsome character. On several occasions, while intoxicated, he threatened the lives of several of the reputable citizens of that city. The details of the crime for which the death penalty was imposed, as near as can be learned, are that he went into a saloon at Gold Roads in which Jennie Bauters was at work and asked her for some money. Upon her refusal to give him the amount of money asked for he drew his gun and fired four shots into her body, any one of which would have proved fatal. He then turned the gun upon himself, but the wound inflicted was only a scratch on the left side near the region of the heart.

On Sunday morning, September 3, 1905, after hours of drinking, Clement headed to Jennie's with a gun in hand. He kicked in her door and demanded the money. She refused, and fearing for her life, she ran outside in her nightgown and bare feet. Jennie didn't get more than 40 feet when Clement shot her in the hip. She begged for her life, begged him not to shoot again, but Clement shot her again. Not a single soul attempted to help Jennie. They heard her screams; - they heard her plead for her life, - but no one stopped this brutal murder.

Clement walked back to the saloon, reloaded his gun, and went back to Jennie lying on the desert pavement and shot her a third and final time in the head. Satisfied she was dead, he turned the gun on himself and fired once into his chest. He then lay down and waited to die, but death did not come. He missed his heart and instead the bullet penetrated his lung and he survived! Clement was arrested, tried, and convicted for the murder of Jennie Bauters. Clement was hanged for her murder on June 18, 1907, in Kingman.

Despite her profession, and what might be thought of her, Jennie was an amazing businesswoman. She amassed a fortune and held the title of Richest Woman in Arizona. She knew she had to protect her assets, so on November 27, 1897, Jennie registered a separate property document under the Registration of Separate Property of a Married Women Act, with the Yavapai County Recorder's Office. This protected all Jennie's assets and everything she had built from anyone claiming they were her husband and entitled to what was rightfully hers alone. But Jennie was unmarried, wasn't she? Maybe she left behind a husband in Belgium. There is no evidence of this as all records show Jennie was unmarried and her actions concerning this remain a mystery.

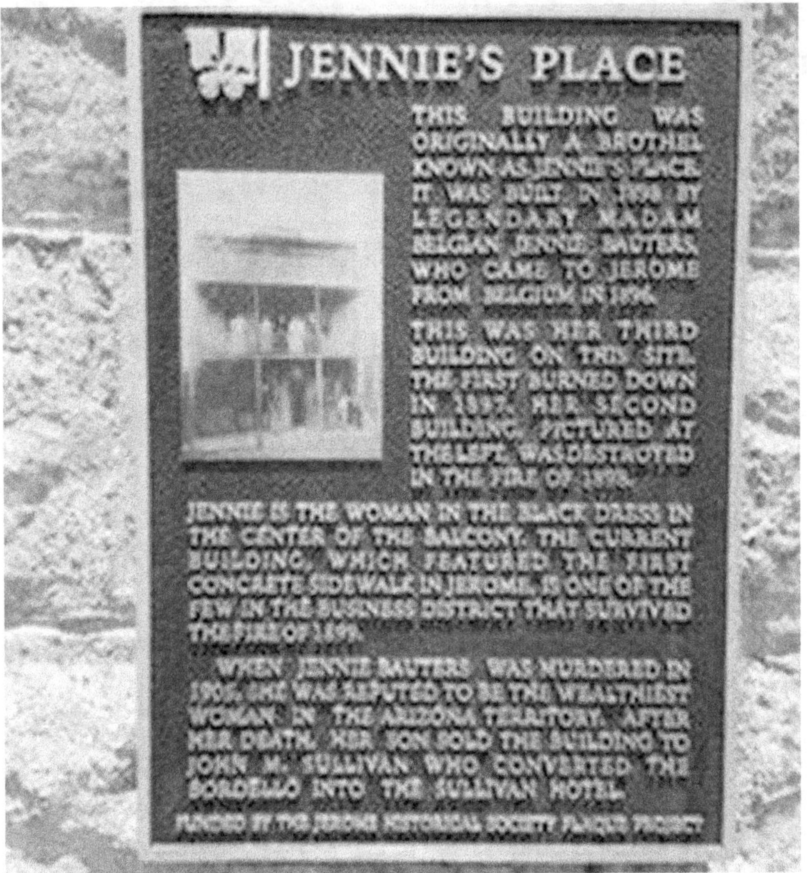

Plaque Marker on the building that was once
"Jennie's Place"

Jennie's son Phillippe was her sole beneficiary and he inherited her entire fortune. He received $14,000.00 and properties she still owned in Jerome. That $14,000 today is valued at $471,181.14, it wasn't pocket change she left for Phillippe.

Until her death, Phillippe did not know his mother's chosen profession. He bought a grave and headstone for her with part of his inheritance.

Jennie was buried in Kingman Pioneer Cemetery. Phillippe then sold the building that was Jennie's Place to John M. Sullivan who converted it into a hotel. Jennie's Place still stands today in Jerome, Arizona; it is now called Nellie Bly, home of the kaleidoscope shop.

The story doesn't end there. Jennie's murderer continues to torment her after both their deaths. Clements was buried in Kingman Pioneer Cemetery, the same as Jenny, but he was in a pauper's grave.

In 1917 the city purchased land for a new cemetery. They contacted surviving families and informed them that their loved ones would be moved from the Kingman Pioneer Cemetery to the new location of Mountain View Cemetery. The families were responsible to pay for the exhumation and reburial of their loved ones. Those bodies that went unclaimed remained where they were. Kingman Pioneer Cemetery was declared abandoned in 1944 and the remaining bodies were piled in a common grave and buried together. Jennie Bauters lies together with her murderer Clement Leigh in that mass grave. under what is now the Lee Williams Stadium, the football field at Kingman High School.

Interestingly Jennie got her start in Jerome from the infamous Madam Nora "Butter" Brown, the real first madam of Jerome. But Nora is a story for another day - she, and her famous customer "Wyatt Earp."

4

Jerome's Haunted Reputation

Today, Jerome is a shadow of its former self. The mines have long since closed and the populations dwindled. But the town's haunted past still lingers on. Prostitute Row, Husband's Alley, and the Jerome Grand Hotel are just some of the haunted places in this town.

The town of Jerome eventually became a ghost town and many of the haunted buildings still stand today. Jerome, Arizona, is a town with a dark past. Once a booming mining town, it eventually became a ghost town after the mines dried up. Still standing today are many of the original buildings from that time.

Are they haunted by the tortured souls of those who once lived there? The live-in maintenance man, among many other spirits, is said to be haunting the Jerome Grand Hotel. The Old Firehouse Inn is also said to be haunted, and guests have reported seeing the ghost of a fireman walking around the property. The Bird Cage Theatre will give you goosebumps. Once a brothel, it is said to be haunted by the ghosts of some of the former employees. Jerome is genuinely a unique- and spooky- experience, so stay awhile and experience the chills.

Jerome Grand Hotel

The most haunted building in Arizona is said to be the Jerome Grand Hotel. This comes as no surprise considering the number of deaths and emotional trauma the building has witnessed - an estimated 9,000 deaths.

The Jerome Grand Hotel was originally the United Verde Hospital, a five-story, 30,000 square ft building with 18-inch-thick concrete walls poured in place on a 50-degree slope. The building could withstand the many mining blasts of up to 260,000 pounds. Constructed in 1927, it was the fourth and final hospital built in Jerome. United Verde Hospital was the most modern hospital in Arizona.

This well-equipped hospital included the Otis self-service elevator - no operator required - one of the first in the country. It serviced all 5 floors of the hospital. The Otis elevator was designed for hospital use as the long, narrow design made it easy to transport wheelchairs, gurneys, and other hospital equipment. The elevator travels at a much slower pace than modern-day elevators, moving only 50 feet per minute versus the normal 800 feet per minute found with today's elevators.

1926 Otis Self-Service Elevator Panel

The hospital was built by the United Verde Copper Mining Company for its many employees and family members at the peak of the population, numbering up to 15,000. Despite the rumors, this hospital was never used as a mental facility nor was it exclusive for tuberculosis patients. It was a general surgical hospital with solid construction, withstanding the mining blasts while other buildings crumbled around it.

The Phelps Dodge Mining Corporation acquired it as part of the United Verde Copper Mine holdings in 1935. They continued to operate and maintain it as a hospital for almost 20 more years.

The hospital closed in 1950 and remained vacant for the next 44 years. Phelps Dodge made the effort to maintain the building even though he recognized it would never again be used as a hospital. Over the years he employed a live-in maintenance man and at times leased it to a family to keep it safe from vandalism. Eventually, it was simply boarded up. Break-ins and vandalism did occur, and with the potential liabilities this caused, Phelps decided to sell.

In May of 1994, Phelps Dodge Corporation sold the hospital to Larry Altherr of Phoenix, Arizona, and he still owns and operates it today. Extensive restoration began almost immediately. Great effort was made to maintain the integrity of both the interior and exterior of this historic building. However, there were some unavoidable changes to be made. When the hospital was built in 1926, very few people drove cars and for the most part horses were more the mode of transportation. The original parking space provided was 12. With the number of tourists and vehicles today that had to be adjusted. Over 1,000 dump truck loads were needed to expand it to 70 parking spaces.

The rooms were ready, and the building reopened in 1996 as the Jerome Grand Hotel. The restaurant opened in 1997 as the Grand View Restaurant and Lounge but soon after, in 2003, it was leased out and opened as the Asylum Restaurant.

The numerous sightings and reports of ghostly encounters and strange events at the Jerome Grand Hotel make it a chilling adventure. Chilling, haunting reports started pouring in almost immediately upon opening. Why wouldn't they; these reports were being voiced when it was still a hospital. Doors opening and closing themselves, chairs moving, items flying off the shelves, calls coming into the front desk from empty rooms, footsteps in the empty hallways, voices, conversations, moaning, and cries of distress. None of this comes from a living source.

This is the story of "Scotty" the most famous ghost at the hotel.

His name was Claude McLeod Harvey, affectionately known as "Scotty" to the town's folk. He was a live-in maintenance man at the United Verde Hospital and rumor has it he was "MURDERED". The official report states his death was accidental, but "Scotty" is hanging around for something that isn't finished yet. Is he looking to have his killer named?

Scotty was born in Aberdeen, Scotland on February 20, 1872. He had been a widower for 6 years before he died on April 3, 1935, from what his death certificate describes as a crushed head as a result of a descending elevator.

Scotty worked on and maintained the 1926 Otis elevator, the same elevator he was pinned under with his head crushed.

Outline of where Claude M Harvey's body was found on that fateful day.

There was a lot of suspicion around his death. The elevator was in perfect working order. It was thoroughly inspected, along with a coroner's inquest, and both determined the elevator did not malfunction - the elevator could not have caused his death. They believed he had been murdered and the body was placed in the elevator shaft to conceal what had really happened.

There are reports of strange noises and lights from the elevator shaft. The creaking iron elevator was heard moving, even when the building was vacant, and there was no electricity. Today, the 1926 Otis self-service elevator continues to move, without requests from a living person throughout the day and night. Employees report the feeling of being watched and seeing a shadowy figure with an angry glare standing in the stairwell. They still hear "Scotty's coughing and sneezing coming from the laundry room.

Claude M. Harvey, "Scotty", is the only undetermined death in the hospital. There have been many theories and suspects. United Verde Copper Company would not allow an autopsy or any x-rays as they did not want suspicion pointing in their direction. Scotty's death was declared an accident. But was it? Accident, murder, or suicide; we may never know, but "Scotty" does, and he is not at rest.

Some say "Scotty" will not rest until his murderer is implicated.

"Scotty" is only one story of Jerome's dark past; there are many more. The Grand Hotel has a lot of mystery, chills, and thrills to share. The town and hotel are said to be home to many ghosts. If you're feeling brave, why not explore Jerome for yourself? You never know what you might find.

5

Jerome Today

Jerome's appearance has changed very little in the last 100 years, with many old buildings still standing.

The remaining residents of Jerome, those stubborn few that remained, protected these historical buildings and kept the town alive. They saved Jerome.

Jerome has clung to life for decades; the town is no longer actively involved in mining. In 1966 the area became a National Historic District and today Jerome has been transformed into an artistic community with a population of 444. It is a tourist attraction receiving more than a million visitors per year. Tourists are drawn to the artists, writers, unique boutiques, bars, and dining spots.

Many of the buildings used by these entrepreneurs are the originals that survived the fires of 1894 and 1899. In the 60s and 70s, artists discovered the ghost town and started trickling in to make it blossom.

Kate Wolf, the American folk singer and songwriter wrote the song "Old Jerome" in 1983. The town council adopted the song as the "official town song" in 1987.

Most recently, police have had to remind locals living in the town that Old West justice should be kept to a minimum. It seems that the locals are fed-up and frustrated with the million tourists visiting their town. The full-time residents are outnumbered 5 to 1 most of the time.

Lately, the residents have been yelling at the tourists and leaving nasty notes on their legally parked vehicles. The residents have been warned this could constitute harassment and have been encouraged to take it up with the police department instead of their current behavior. Jerome relies on these tourists to sustain its economy. This is not the impression to make on the very people keeping your town alive.

The tourists come to Jerome to enjoy the many fun things to do in this historic landmark; embarking upon an adventure through downtown ruins where visible reminders of our country's natural resources still exist despite progress.

There are many locations of interest, such as the Douglas Mansion Museum and State Park. In the Gold King Mine, you can walk through and view the mining gear used to excavate the many riches of the town. The old Sliding Jail and Glass Viewing Platform at Audrey Headframe Park and the Jerome Grant Hotel are rumored to be haunted.

Jerome is a town with a rich history full of exciting stories and characters. Whether you're interested in its mining past or its haunted present, there's something for everyone in this book of Jerome, Arizona: The Wickedest Town in the Wild West.

6

Resources

Mining Town Archive. (n.d.). WESTERN MINING HISTORY. Western Mining History. Retrieved September 19, 2022, from https://westernmininghistory.com/towns/arizona/jerome/

AZGS. (1952, July). Story of The United Verde. Arizona Department of Mineral Resources. Retrieved September 19, 2022, from http://docs.azgs.az.gov/OnlineAccessMineFiles/Pubs/2013-02-0386.pdf

SGHA. (n.d.). Report Prostitution Row, Husband's Alley. SGHA.Net. Retrieved September 19, 2022, from http://www.sgha.net/az/Prostitution_Row.pdf

RobRob. (2015, April 14). Jerome, Arizona: The Wickedest Town in the West! TravelLatte. Retrieved September 19, 2022, from http://travellatte.net/jerome-arizona-the-wickedest-town-in-the-west/

Ron Dungan. (2016, May 27). Inglorious Arizona: Belgian Jennie, the madam of Jerome, was more than a myth. Azcentral. Retrieved

September 19, 2022, from https://www.azcentral.com/story/news/local/arizona-best-reads/2016/03/09/inglorious-arizona-belgian-jennie-madam-jerome-more-than-myth/81451438/

Monroe, H. (2021, December 12). The Murder of Jennie Bauters -. Medium. Retrieved September 19, 2022, from https://heathermonroe.medium.com/the-murder-of-jennie-bauters-ae1b11006d0c

Lieberman, H. (2018, June 21). A Short History of the Condom. JSTOR Daily. Retrieved September 19, 2022, from https://daily.jstor.org/short-history-of-the-condom/

History of Jerome - One of the best hotels in Arizona. (n.d.). Retrieved September 19, 2022, from https://jeromegrandhotel.net/jerome-history/